THE ELEMENTS

Carbon

Giles Sparrow

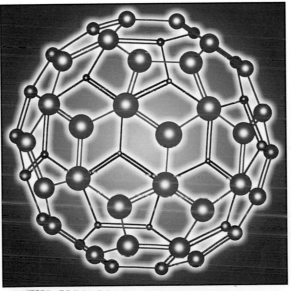

BENCHMARK BOOKS

MARSHALL CAVENDISH

NEW YORK

Benchmark Books
Marshall Cavendish Corporation
99 White Plains Road
Tarrytown, New York 10591-9001

Library of Congress Cataloging-in-Publication Data
Sparrow, Giles.
Carbon / by Giles Sparrow.
p.   cm. — (The elements)
Includes index.
Summary: Discusses the origin, discovery, special characteristics, and uses of carbon.
ISBN 0-7614-0878-9 (lib. bdg.)
1. Carbon—Juvenile literature. [1. Carbon.] I. Title. II. Series: Elements
(Benchmark Books)
QD181.C1S65 1999
546'.681—dc21   97-36423 CIP AC

Printed in Hong Kong

Picture credits
Corbis (UK) Ltd: 3, 9, 11, 12, 13, 16, 20.
Mary Evans Picture Library: 10.
Science Photo Library: 4, 6, 8, 14, 15, 17, 18, 19, 21, 22, 23, 24, 25, 26, 27, 30.

Series created by Brown Packaging Partworks
Designed by wda

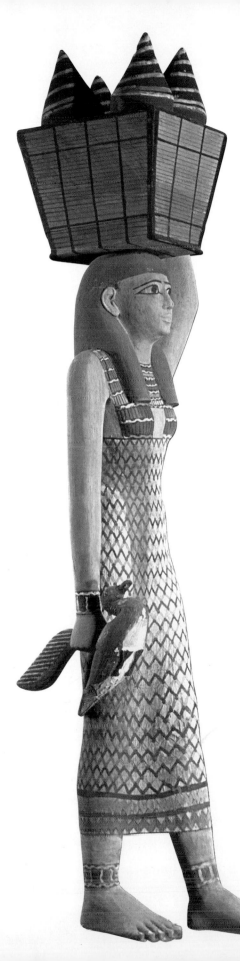

Contents

What is carbon?

hat do a sparkling diamond and a lump of coal have in common? They are both forms of carbon. Carbon is perhaps the most important of all the elements, because the chemicals that create life are based on it.

Anywhere you look in the world, you can find carbon and materials that contain it. It is locked away in limestone rocks, floating in the air as carbon dioxide, hidden underground in coal and oil, and on its own as diamonds and graphite (pencil lead).

Carbon in the periodic table

Carbon is found in Group IV of the periodic table and has atomic number 6. All elements are made up of tiny units called atoms, which can only be seen using extremely powerful microscopes. Inside the atoms are minute particles: positively charged protons, negatively charged electrons, and neutrons, which do not have any charge. The atomic number tells us how many protons there are in each atom of an element, so carbon atoms contain six protons.

Inside the atom

The protons cluster together with the neutrons in the nucleus in the center of the atom. The number of protons in each atom is balanced by the number of electrons. There are six electrons inside a carbon atom, which move around the nucleus in shells. Two of carbon's electrons are locked away in a small inner shell. The other four are in an outer shell, which can hold up to eight electrons.

A stable arrangement

Atoms are only stable if their outer electron shell is full. They gain, lose, or share electrons with other atoms so that all

This sparkling diamond is one of the naturally occurring forms of carbon.

the atoms involved end up with complete outer shells. As the atoms transfer or share electrons in a reaction, they form bonds between each other, resulting in molecules and compounds.

Carbon and its compounds

Carbon is very reactive. It forms a huge number of compounds with many other elements. Compounds containing carbon outnumber the compounds of all the other elements. The study of organic, or carbon-based, chemistry is one of the most important areas of science.

As well as joining with other elements, carbon atoms can also form strong bonds with up to four other carbon atoms. This produces rings or chains, which can be many thousands of atoms long.

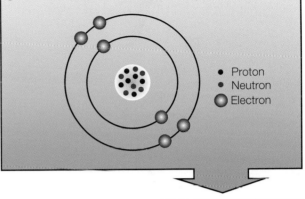

ATOMS AT WORK

Each element has an atomic mass, which is the number of protons and neutrons added together. Carbon has six protons and six neutrons. This gives it an atomic mass of 12.

- Proton
- Neutron
- Electron

But there is also an unusual form of carbon, which has eight neutrons in its nucleus. This special form is called an isotope. It has the same atomic number as the normal form of carbon, but its atomic mass is 14. The extra mass makes the nucleus unstable. It breaks apart, giving off radioactivity.

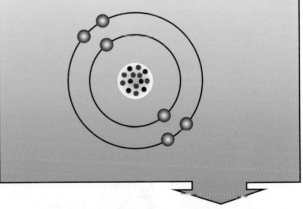

Scientists measure the radioactivity and use it to find the age of objects that contain dead plant or animal material. This process is called carbon dating (see page 13). It has been used to find the age of wooden ornaments, boats that have lain at the bottom of the ocean for hundreds of years, and the remains of prehistoric plants, animals, and people.

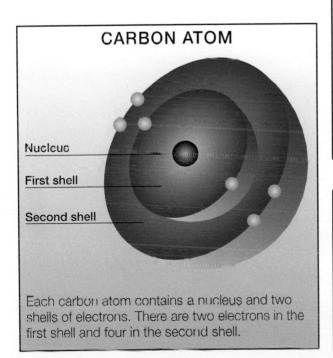

CARBON ATOM

Nucleus

First shell

Second shell

Each carbon atom contains a nucleus and two shells of electrons. There are two electrons in the first shell and four in the second shell.

The "lead" inside pencils is not made of lead but of graphite. Graphite is a soft, flaky form of carbon.

Carbon also has three crystalline forms, in which each atom bonds with its neighbors to create a regular, repeating pattern. Two of these forms have been known for many hundreds of years. The third has only recently been discovered, and scientists are still finding out about its properties and possible uses. These different crystalline forms are called allotropes of carbon.

Different forms

Although most of the world's carbon is bound up in compounds with other elements, carbon does exist on its own. The most common form is amorphous (shapeless) carbon. This is lumps of carbon without any overall structure, such as coal and charcoal.

Rings and planes

The most common allotrope is graphite, which is used to make the "lead" in pencils. In graphite, each carbon atom forms three links with its neighbors in a single flat plane. These carbon atoms form hexagonal rings.

Because carbon atoms have four electrons to share, each carbon atom still has one bond left to make. It is this bond that holds the material together. Alternate sheets form links with each other, but these links are much weaker than the normal bonds in the flat plane. The weak bonds break easily, allowing the planes to slide past each other.

Four strong bonds

The next allotrope is diamond, the hardest natural substance on Earth. It is the bonding between the carbon atoms in diamond that give it its hardness.

In a diamond molecule, each atom is joined to four others in a tetrahedron around it. All the bonds have the same strength, and the regular pattern through the diamond makes it extremely hard.

Diamonds can only be split by an expert who knows where to find a point called the plane of cleavage. This is the place where all of the bonds line up across the diamond.

ATOMS AT WORK

The carbon atoms in graphite are arranged in flat rings. Each carbon atom is linked, or bonded, to three other carbon atoms. Three of the electrons in each atom are taken up in a chemical bond. The fourth electron is free to move around the whole structure. The flat rings are held together weakly, so they easily slide past one another.

Graphite

In a diamond, each carbon atom makes four strong bonds with four other carbon atoms. The atoms are arranged in a shape called a tetrahedron. The strong bonds make diamond very hard. In fact, it is the hardest known natural substance.

Diamond

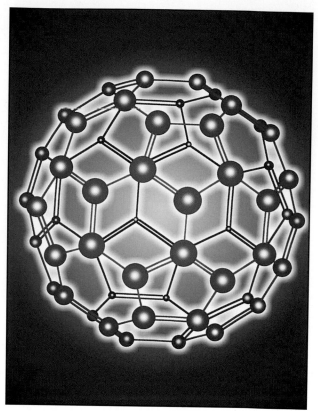

This is a computer model of buckminsterfullerene, a natural form of carbon made of 60 atoms. Buckminsterfullerene was discovered in 1990.

Fullerenes—a new discovery

Recently, a new type of carbon, called the fullerene, has been discovered. Fullerenes are large molecules with many carbon atoms linked in hexagons and pentagons. The surface of the molecule looks like a soccer ball. The most famous, buckminsterfullerene, has 60 carbon atoms. Other fullerenes contain anything from 28 to 70 carbon atoms.

These industrial diamonds are prized more for their hardness than for their appearance.

Where carbon is found

When the universe began, it contained only the lightest elements, hydrogen and helium. All the other elements that exist today, including carbon, were created from hydrogen and helium. In the intense heat inside stars, atoms of hydrogen and helium joined together in different combinations to make heavier elements. Carbon is one of the more widespread heavy elements—it may make up almost 0.5 percent of the universe's mass.

Carbon on Earth

Our solar system formed from material that was quite rich in carbon. Even so, the element only makes up 0.025 percent of Earth's crust, and most of this carbon is bound up in rocks and minerals such as limestone and chalk. But carbon is highly concentrated in living creatures and accounts for nearly one-quarter of the atoms in our tissues.

Graphite is the commonest form of crystalline carbon found on Earth. Diamond is much rarer. It is found in places where graphite has been compressed underground at high temperatures and pressures. Most of the world's diamonds are found in Russia, South Africa, and South America. Recently, some natural fullerenes have been found in Siberia, Russia, locked away in a rare mineral called shungite.

Much of the carbon on Earth is locked away in rocks, such as the ones in this limestone cave.

Early people burned charcoal in furnaces to melt iron compounds so they could extract and use the metal.

How carbon was discovered

People have known about carbon since prehistoric times, although it was only identified as an element in the 18th century, when the science of chemistry began to develop. Our ancestors were using charcoal as long ago as 1,000 B.C.E. These early people found that burning charcoal with iron ore (iron mixed with oxygen) left behind the pure iron metal, which they fashioned into tools and weapons. Carbon's name comes from a Latin word *carbo*, which means "charcoal."

Diamonds and graphite

The ancient Greeks knew about diamonds and used them for their hardness. The word diamond comes from the Greek for "unconquerable." For centuries, all diamonds came from India. They were found in riverbeds where the force of the water had washed them out of the surrounding rock. Diamond mining began much later, when diamonds were discovered under the ground in South Africa and South America.

Graphite is a natural part of the landscape in many areas. Large deposits are found in Madagascar, Mexico, and Sri Lanka. But it was only put into use in the 1500s, with the invention of the pencil.

DID YOU KNOW?

FINDING FULLERENES

Fullerenes are the only form of carbon that has been discovered by modern scientists. They were found by a group of scientists trying to explain large carbon molecules they had detected in distant space. The scientists wanted to find out what these molecules were. They heated graphite with a laser until it formed a vapor. When the vapor cooled down again, it solidified into fullerenes.

Using carbon

As well as being vital to life on Earth and an important source of energy, carbon is widely used in industry. Without it, modern life would be very different.

As we have seen, one of the earliest uses of carbon was in smelting iron. Charcoal forms when wood burns without a supply of air. It is very good at removing oxygen from other materials.

In the 1700s, people started to use coke instead of charcoal. Coke forms when coal burns without air. It is much easier to make than charcoal but is just as good at removing oxygen from things. Coke is still used today in furnaces for extracting metals from their ores.

Amorphous carbon has useful properties. Short strands of carbon are called carbon fibers. Carbon fibers are very tough. They are mixed with plastics to make materials that are as strong as most metals but much lighter. Carbon fibers are used to make tennis rackets, skis, and the shells of racing cars.

Hard and beautiful

Although diamonds are very expensive and popular as gemstones, only a very few stones are of high enough quality for

Carbon fibers are extremely strong but lightweight, which makes them the perfect material for making racing car bodies.

jewelry. The others are used for their hardness. Small diamonds are used on drills and cutters. Artificial diamonds, made by heating graphite under very high pressure, are also used in industry.

A slippery substance

Graphite is used mainly for its unusual properties. Layers slip off the surface as you touch it, and this makes graphite an excellent lubricating agent.

Moving parts in a machine rub against each other, causing friction. Eventually this rubbing wears the parts out. A layer of graphite between the moving parts makes the machine last longer. The parts slide past the slippery graphite and do not rub against one another.

Graphite is also used as a electrical conductor and as the "lead" in pencils.

Fullerenes

Fullerenes might prove to be one of the most useful forms of carbon. Scientists are studying fullerene superconductors—substances that conduct electricity perfectly.

This sidewalk artist is using charcoal. Sadly, his picture will be washed away by the next shower of rain.

Carbon dating

Ot important use of carbon is carbon dating. Carbon atoms exist in two forms, or isotopes. The normal form is carbon-12. The less common form is carbon-14. The nucleus in an atom of carbon-14 has extra neutrons, which make it unstable. It decays, giving off radioactivity, which can be measured with an instrument called a Geiger counter.

Exchanging carbon

Throughout their lives, all living creatures exchange carbon with the environment.

This ancient Egyptian wooden figure dates from 2,000 B.C.E. Scientists used carbon dating to calculate its age.

> **DID YOU KNOW?**
>
> **DATING STONEHENGE**
> One of carbon dating's greatest successes has been dating the great stone circle at Stonehenge in England. The stones do not contain any carbon, but archaeologists have found many items—tools, plants, and even buried bodies—that date from the same time. By carbon dating this material, they now know that building work began around 3,100 b.c.e. Before this discovery, they thought Stonehenge had been copied from Greek monuments a thousand years younger.

As long as they are alive, the proportion of carbon-14 in their bodies is the same as in the environment as a whole. When a plant or animal dies, it stops absorbing carbon from the atmosphere, and radioactive decay slowly reduces the proportion of carbon-14 it contains.

A steady rate of decay

The decay of carbon-14 atoms is very useful to scientists who want to find how old something is. Radioactive decay happens at a steady rate. Scientists know that it takes 5,730 years for half the atoms of carbon-14 in a sample of material to decay. This time is called the half-life. By measuring the number of carbon atoms left in a piece of plant or animal material, scientists can work out how long ago the living creature died.

Coal, oil, and gas

Most of the world's energy needs are provided by burning carbon. Carbon-rich fuels include coal, oil, and natural gas. They are known as fossil fuels because they were formed millions of years ago from dead plants and animals.

How coal formed

During the Carboniferous Period, 300 million years ago, Earth looked very different than it does today. The land was covered with swamps and forests. The climate was warm and wet all year round,

The coal we burn today began to form 300 million years ago in the swampy forests that covered Earth.

and plants grew quickly. When the plants died and fell to the ground, they became covered with layers of mud and soil. As more layers piled on top, the dead plants eventually hardened into coal.

Types of coal

There are three types of coal, depending on how much carbon they contain. The more carbon there is in the coal, and the more it was compressed, the harder and blacker it becomes.

The softest coal is lignite. This is brown, and you can still see chunks of wood in it. Bituminous coal is black and crumbly. It burns easily. The hardest type is anthracite, which formed under high heat and pressure. It is hard to ignite and burns with a smokeless flame.

Coal is mined from seams, or beds, which are found at different depths below Earth's surface. In the United States, there are enormous coal beds in the Appalachian region, Arkansas, Illinois, Indiana, Iowa, Kansas, Kentucky, Missouri, Oklahoma, and parts of Texas.

Anthracite, or high-grade coal, is very hard and black. It contains 85 to 98 percent carbon.

DID YOU KNOW?

POLLUTING THE ENVIRONMENT

Coal does not contain pure carbon. The carbon is mixed with other elements, including oxygen, nitrogen, and sulfur. Whenever coal is burned, these elements are released into the air as sulfur and nitrogen oxides.

Burning coal is a major cause of acid rain. The sulfur oxides and nitrogen oxides dissolve in rainwater to form acids. When the acid rain falls to Earth, it kills plants, pollutes rivers, and damages buildings.

ATOMS AT WORK

When coal burns in air, the carbon in the coal reacts with the oxygen in the air.

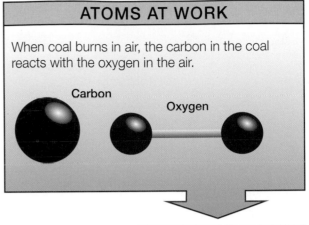

The bonds holding the oxygen molecules break apart, and the oxygen atoms are free to form new bonds.

Two oxygen atoms become attached to an atom of carbon to form carbon dioxide. Carbon dioxide gas is released into the atmosphere.

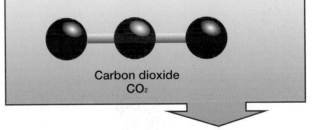

Carbon dioxide
CO_2

The reaction that takes place when coal burns can be written like this:

$C + O_2 \rightarrow CO_2$

This shows that one atom of carbon reacts with a molecule of oxygen to form one molecule of carbon dioxide.

A "nodding donkey" drilling for oil at Huntington Beach, California.

How oil formed

Oil is the remains of tiny creatures that lived in the prehistoric oceans. When these creatures died, their bodies sank to the ocean floor. The remains decayed a little, but decay needs oxygen, which the still waters did not supply.

As mud and more dead matter fell to the seabed, the remains were crushed under their own weight. Eventually they turned into a liquid, known as crude oil.

Sometimes, the liquid oil stays mixed with the muddy "sediment," creating a rock called oil shale. But if the conditions are right, the oil can rise up through the sediment, forming a deposit of liquid oil. Because oil forms underwater, it is usually found by drilling the ocean floor or land that was once covered by the sea.

Oil refining

Crude oil is really a mixture of different chemicals called hydrocarbons. Each of the hydrocarbons has a particular use.

After the crude oil has been brought to the surface, it is processed to separate the hydrocarbons. This process is called refining. Refining is based on the fact that each hydrocarbon boils (turns to vapor) at a different temperature. The crude oil is heated until it vaporizes. The vapor is pumped into a tower, which is hot at the bottom and cooler toward the top.

As the vapors rise up the tower, they cool and turn back into liquid. The different hydrocarbons turn to liquid at different temperatures and at different levels in the tower. They can be collected and tapped off. The lightest fractions float out of the top of the tower as gas.

OIL FACTS

● At present, the worldwide use of oil is 24 billion barrels a year. Each barrel holds 42 gallons (160 liters).

● Fossil fuels will all run out eventually. The world's known oil reserves will last 40 years, but it is hoped that undiscovered resources may last for up to a century. Coal reserves will last much longer.

● More than half the world's oil reserves are found in just four countries: Saudi Arabia, Iraq, Kuwait, and Iran.

The carbon cycle

There is only a limited amount of carbon in Earth's environment, and it is needed for the chemical processes that support life. So carbon is constantly cycling around Earth, turning up in lots of different forms and places. The reactions that move carbon around make a giant web, called the carbon cycle.

Plants get carbon by taking carbon dioxide from the air. They use the carbon dioxide and the energy from sunlight to make food. This process is called photosynthesis. Animals get their carbon by eating plants or other animals.

Carbon dioxide returns to the atmosphere when plants and animals breathe. When organisms breathe, they take oxygen from the air. The oxygen reacts with food to provide energy. This is called respiration. It produces carbon dioxide, which is released to the air.

Volcanic eruptions are another source of carbon. When a volcano erupts, it releases massive amounts of carbon dioxide. But the effect of volcanoes is balanced by

Green plants take carbon dioxide from the atmosphere and use it to make food.

weathering. This is a chemical reaction between rainwater and rocks that absorbs carbon dioxide from the air to create rock carbonate minerals.

Upsetting the cycle

Left to themselves, these natural processes are in perfect balance. But many people are worried that human activities are disturbing the cycle and increasing the amount of carbon dioxide in the atmosphere. This could cause problems in the future, because carbon dioxide is vital for controlling the world's climate.

CARBON CYCLE FACTS

● All the living creatures on Earth contain from 660 billion to 1,100 billion tons (600 billion to 1,000 billion tonnes) of carbon.

● There are about 770 billion tons (700 billion tonnes) of carbon in the atmosphere.

● Burning fossil fuels currently adds about 6 billion tons (5.4 billion tonnes) of carbon to the atmosphere each year.

The eruption of Mount St. Helens on July 22, 1980 threw masses of carbon dioxide into the air.

The greenhouse effect

Like the glass in a greenhouse, carbon dioxide in Earth's atmosphere traps heat. Without this so-called greenhouse effect, all the heat from Earth's surface would escape into space and Earth would be far too cold for anything to survive.

Many people are worried that the amount of carbon dioxide in the atmosphere is getting too high. As a result, Earth is getting hotter and hotter, leading to global warming.

Global warming

The effects of global warming could be catastrophic. As the world's temperature heats up, the ice caps and ice fields of the frozen polar regions will melt. The oceans will expand, flooding low-lying land. The raised temperatures will cause droughts. Crops will fail and there will be famines in many parts of the world.

Human activities are to blame

Two main activities are responsible for upsetting the natural greenhouse effect. First, burning fossil fuels releases carbon dioxide gas into the atmosphere. Second, all across the world, forests are being cut down to make way for houses, roads, and farmland. But trees play an important part in the carbon cycle by taking carbon dioxide from the air for photosynthesis. The loss of all these trees makes the problem worse.

The carbon cycle may help slow the effect. The warmer climate will cause more rain. This would increase the weathering on rocks, absorbing more carbon dioxide. But if we continue to rely on fossil fuels as our main energy source, the climate may eventually be changed beyond recovery.

Rainforests in many parts of the world are being burned to clear the ground for roads and farmland.

How carbon reacts

Carbon reacts with oxygen to form one of two gases. These are carbon dioxide and carbon monoxide. Carbon dioxide is created when carbon burns with a steady supply of air. Each carbon atom forms bonds with two oxygen atoms. If the burning takes place in a limited air supply, however, the carbon atom binds with only one oxygen atom, forming carbon monoxide.

Metal carbides

Carbon will react with metals if it is heated to very high temperatures in a furnace. The reaction produces compounds called metal carbides. Some carbides have useful properties. Tungsten carbide, for

Frozen carbon dioxide is used in theaters and at rock concerts to create a smoky effect.

DID YOU KNOW?

WHAT MAKES DRINKS FIZZ?
Just as solids such as sugar can dissolve in water, so can gases. Carbon dioxide is dissolved into many soft drinks to give them their fizz. The gas is bubbled through the drink under pressure, which makes it dissolve better into the liquid than it would normally. The drink is sealed up at the same pressure, keeping the gas dissolved in the drink. When the can is opened, this pressure is released. The carbon dioxide gas bubbles out and makes the drink fizz.

example, is used in high-speed cutting tools. The compound is very hard and remains stable even at the high temperatures the tools operate at.

Carbonates

Compounds combining carbon, oxygen, and metal atoms are called carbonates. They form when a metal reacts with carbonic acid, a weak acid created when carbon dioxide dissolves in water.

Carbonates can be made in a laboratory but also form in nature when rain falls on rock. Calcium carbonate, better known as chalk or limestone, is the most common of these compounds.

Reactions with hydrogen

The most varied group of carbon compounds are those that involve hydrogen. The simplest of these are the hydrocarbons where the carbon atoms are bonded only to other carbons or to hydrogen atoms.

The simplest hydrocarbon is methane (chemical formula CH_4), which is the main ingredient of natural gas. It has one carbon atom attached to four hydrogen atoms. Other hydrocarbons are larger and more complicated. But there is a whole range of other compounds, and a separate field, organic chemistry, is devoted to studying them (see page 24).

Stalagmites and stalactites form when calcium carbonate drips from the ceiling of a limestone cave.

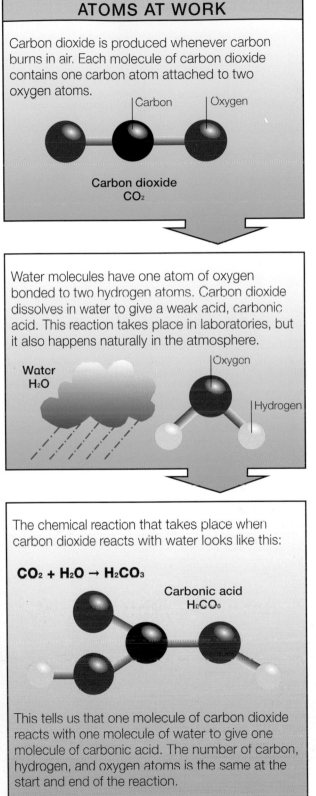

ATOMS AT WORK

Carbon dioxide is produced whenever carbon burns in air. Each molecule of carbon dioxide contains one carbon atom attached to two oxygen atoms.

Carbon   Oxygen

Carbon dioxide
CO_2

Water molecules have one atom of oxygen bonded to two hydrogen atoms. Carbon dioxide dissolves in water to give a weak acid, carbonic acid. This reaction takes place in laboratories, but it also happens naturally in the atmosphere.

Water
H_2O

Oxygen

Hydrogen

The chemical reaction that takes place when carbon dioxide reacts with water looks like this:

$CO_2 + H_2O \rightarrow H_2CO_3$

Carbonic acid
H_2CO_3

This tells us that one molecule of carbon dioxide reacts with one molecule of water to give one molecule of carbonic acid. The number of carbon, hydrogen, and oxygen atoms is the same at the start and end of the reaction.

Carbon in the body

Carbon is the main ingredient of all the tissues inside living creatures. The large number of bonds each carbon atom can make allow it to build up the huge molecules, with complex functions, needed for life. There are three main types of carbon-based compounds in plants and animals: carbohydrates, fats, and proteins.

Carbon-containing compounds provide the energy these marathon runners need to complete their race.

Carbohydrates

Carbohydrates make up a large part of our diet. They include sugars such as glucose and sucrose, which are broken down inside the body to release energy. Other carbohydrates are cellulose, the main building material in plants, and starch, which plants and animals use for storing energy.

Fats

Fats are like an energy bank. When we eat more food than we need, the extra material is converted to fats and stored.

Foods that are rich in carbohydrates include cereals, pasta, and bread.

Later, if our bodies need more energy than they get from our diet, the fat molecules are broken down to release energy. Fats can store more energy than carbohydrates in a smaller space. Fats are also good at keeping the body warm. Animals such as walruses and polar bears, which swim in frozen Arctic waters, have a thick layer of fat beneath their skin.

Proteins

Proteins are the most complex of the three major groups. Each protein molecule is made of hundreds of thousands of smaller molecules called amino acids linked together in a chain. There are 20 amino acids, which combine to give a huge variety of protein molecules, all with different and distinctive properties.

Nearly all our bodily parts are made of proteins, including skin, muscle, and our internal organs. Some protein molecules are enzymes, which drive the chemical reactions inside the body that keep us alive. Other proteins—called DNA—are like recipe books, carrying the detailed instructions that tell cells how to make all the proteins a living organism needs throughout its life.

Organic compounds are used in a variety of substances, including detergent bubbles!

organic chemical urea, which is produced in the body as a waste product.

Today, organic compounds are an important part of the modern world. They include gasoline, fabrics, dyes, detergents, drugs, and plastics. A world without carbon compounds is impossible to imagine.

Organic chemistry

Scientists have identified more than 6 million compounds that contain carbon. The number of these compounds is so enormous that a separate field of chemistry is devoted to studying them. This area is called organic chemistry.

Organic chemistry got its name because early chemists thought that carbon compounds only existed in plants and animals. These scientists thought the compounds contained a special life-giving substance and could not be made in a laboratory. This changed in 1828, when German scientist Friedrich Wöhler (1800–1882) managed to create the

A unique property

The reason there are so many compounds is the unique ability of carbon atoms to form strong bonds with other carbon atoms. The simplest organic molecule has one carbon atom, while more complicated compounds contain hundreds of thousands of carbon atoms.

The carbon atoms in organic compounds also make bonds with other elements, including hydrogen, oxygen, nitrogen, and sulfur.

Compounds that contain only carbon and hydrogen are called hydrocarbons. The simplest is methane, which has one carbon atom and four hydrogen atoms (CH_4). The hydrocarbons build up as more carbon atoms are added. After methane comes ethane (C_2H_6), then propane (C_3H_8) and butane (C_4H_{10}). More complicated hydrocarbons can contain double or triple bonds between some of the carbons in the chain.

Joining in a ring

When six carbon atoms join together in a ring, this makes a substance called benzene. On its own, benzene is a poisonous oily liquid. But benzene can form a part of other compounds, many of which are useful. Some have pleasant smells and are used to make perfumes. In fact, all compounds that contain a benzene ring are called aromatic.

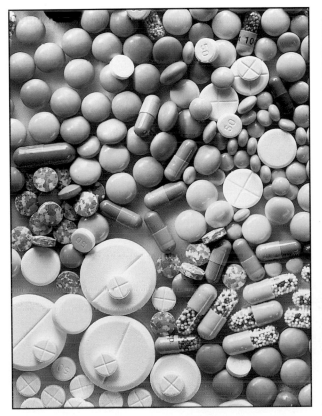

Many of the drugs doctors use to fight disease are made from carbon-containing compounds.

ATOMS AT WORK

Butane is the simplest hydrocarbon that has isomers. Isomers are molecules that have the same number of atoms, but the atoms are arranged in different ways.

Butane contains four carbon atoms and ten hydrogen atoms. In the first isomer, the carbon atoms are arranged in a straight chain. This isomer is named n-butane.

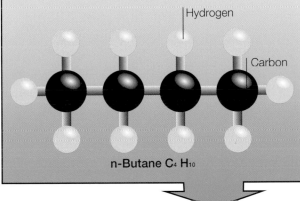

n-Butane C_4H_{10}

In the second isomer, three carbon atoms are arranged in a line. The fourth carbon atom doesn't join the end of the chain. Instead, it attaches to the middle carbon in the line. This isomer has a different structure and a different name—isobutane.

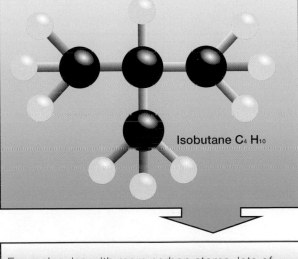

Isobutane C_4H_{10}

For molecules with more carbon atoms, lots of different arrangements are possible and the isomers become more complicated.

Polymers

What does a hair from your head have in common with a plastic sheet? They are both made of polymers, a special type of organic compound.

Polymers are giant molecules. They are made of smaller molecules, called monomers, joined together in a long chain. A single polymer chain can contain hundreds, thousands, or even millions of monomer units. The monomers can all be the same, or there can be two or more different monomers joined together in a regular pattern.

The polymer chains are held together by links between the monomer units. The way the polymer molecules line up depends on these links. Polymer chains that line up close together in regular rows make hard, solid materials. Other polymers are tangled and irregular. This makes a material flexible and rubbery.

Important polymers

Polymers are everywhere. Natural polymers include silk, cotton, wool, starch, and rubber. The proteins that build bodily cells are polymer molecules. So too are the DNA molecules that tell our cells how to make new proteins.

Most of the polymer materials we use today are artificial. They are made from substances called petrochemicals, by-products of oil refining.

Among the most remarkable polymers are plastics. The name comes from a Greek word meaning "easy to shape." This gives us a clue about their properties—plastics soften when they are heated and can be molded into different shapes. Once they harden, they form materials that are strong but lightweight. Plastics do not rot, like wood, or rust, like metal.

We use plastics every day. Familiar ones include: polyester, which makes clothing; polyethylene, which is used in plastic bags and squeeze bottles; and Teflon, the nonstick coating on frying pans.

A range of plastic containers. Plastic is one of the most widely used of all artificial polymers.

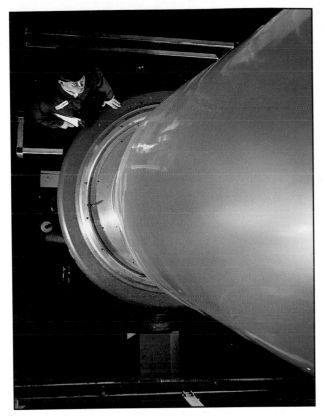

This machine makes polyethylene sheets from recycled waste products.

ATOMS AT WORK

Polyethylene is made of ethene molecules joined together in a long chain. The carbon atoms in the ethene molecule are held together by a strong double bond.

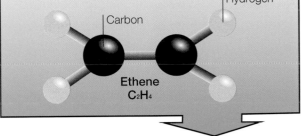

Hydrogen

Carbon

Ethene
C_2H_4

It takes a lot of energy to break the strong bond, so the ethene is heated and put under high pressure. The bond breaks, and the molecule divides into two fragments. These are called radicals, and they are very reactive.

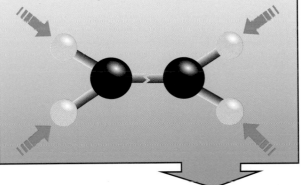

The reaction is written: $C_2H_4 \rightarrow C_nH_{(2n + 2)}$

Because we don't know how long the polyethylene molecule is, we use the letter n instead of a number to show how many atoms it contains.

Polyethylene $C_nH_{(2n+2)}$

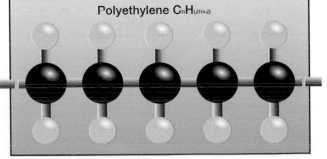

POLYMER FACTS

● Rubber is a natural polymer with flexible bonds that allow the material to be stretched and then return to its original shape.

● Plastics are polymers that curl up and become tangled with each other when they are cooled. Some plastics are thermoplastic—they uncurl when they are heated again. Others are thermosetting—they solidify as they cool and cannot be melted again.

● Kevlar is a plastic that is stronger than steel but much lighter. It is used in airplane parts and to make bullet-proof vests.

Periodic table

Everything in the universe is made from combinations of substances called elements. Elements are the building blocks of matter. They are made of tiny atoms, which are much too small to see.

The character of an atom depends on how many even tinier particles called protons there are in its center, or nucleus. An element's atomic number is the same as the number of protons.

Scientists have found around 110 different elements. About 90 elements occur naturally on Earth. The rest have been made in experiments.

All these elements are set out on a chart called the periodic table. This lists all the elements in order according to their atomic number.

The elements at the left of the table are metals. Those at the right are nonmetals. Between the metals and the nonmetals are the metalloids, which sometimes act like metals and sometimes like nonmetals.

● On the left of the table are the alkali metals. These elements have just one electron in their outer shells.

● On the right of the periodic table are the noble gases. These elements have full outer shells.

● Elements in the same group have the same number of electrons in their outer shells.

● Elements get more reactive as you go down a group.

● The number of electrons orbiting the nucleus increases down each group.

● The transition metals are in the middle of the table, between Groups II and III.

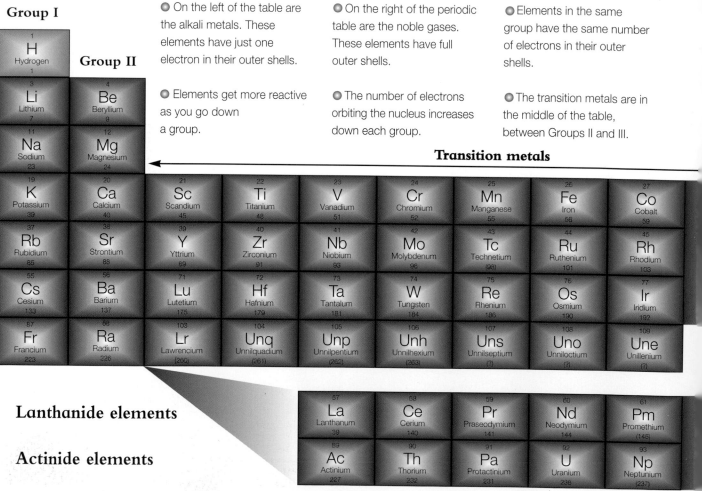

Group I

Group II

Transition metals

Lanthanide elements

Actinide elements

The horizontal rows are called periods. As you go across a period, the atomic number increases by one from each element to the next. The vertical columns are called groups. Elements get heavier as you go down a group. All the elements in a group have the same number of electrons in their outer shells. This means they react in similar ways.

The transition metals fall between Groups II and III. Their electron shells fill up in an unusual way. The lanthanide elements and the actinide elements are set apart from the main table to make it easier to read. All the lanthanide elements and the actinide elements are quite rare.

Carbon in the table

Carbon has atomic number six, so it has six protons in its nucleus. It is in Group IV, which means there are four electrons in its outer shell. Carbon reacts with metals and nonmetals to form a huge number of compounds. Its chemical reactions are similar to those of silicon, which is directly below carbon in Group IV.

Metals

Metalloids (semimetals)

Nonmetals

6
C
Carbon
12

Atomic (proton) number
Symbol
Name
Atomic mass

Group VIII

Group III	Group IV	Group V	Group VI	Group VII	2 He Helium 4
5 B Boron 11	6 C Carbon 12	7 N Nitrogen 14	8 O Oxygen 16	9 F Fluorine 19	10 Ne Neon 20
13 Al Aluminum 27	14 Si Silicon 28	15 P Phosphorus 31	16 S Sulfur 32	17 Cl Chlorine 35	18 Ar Argon 40

28 Ni Nickel 59	29 Cu Copper 64	30 Zn Zinc 65	31 Ga Gallium 70	32 Ge Germanium 73	33 As Arsenic 75	34 Se Selenium 79	35 Br Bromine 80	36 Kr Krypton 84
46 Pd Palladium 106	47 Ag Silver 108	48 Cd Cadmium 112	49 In Indium 115	50 Sn Tin 119	51 Sb Antimony 122	52 Te Tellurium 128	53 I Iodine 127	54 Xe Xenon 131
78 Pt Platinum 195	79 Au Gold 197	80 Hg Mercury 201	81 Tl Thallium 204	82 Pb Lead 207	83 Bi Bismuth 209	84 Po Polonium (209)	85 At Astatine (210)	86 Rn Radon (222)

62 Sm Samarium 150	63 Eu Europium 152	64 Gd Gadolinium 157	65 Tb Terbium 159	66 Dy Dysprosium 163	67 Ho Holmium 165	68 Er Erbium 167	69 Tm Thulium 169	70 Yb Ytterbium 173
94 Pu Plutonium (244)	95 Am Americium (243)	96 Cm Curium (247)	97 Bk Berkelium (247)	98 Cf Californium (251)	99 Es Einsteinium (252)	100 Fm Fermium (257)	101 Md Mendelevium (258)	102 No Nobelium (259)

Chemical reactions

Chemical reactions are going on around us all the time. Some reactions involve just two substances; others many more. But whenever a reaction takes place, at least one substance is changed.

In a chemical reaction, the atoms stay the same. But they join up in different combinations to form new molecules.

Writing an equation

Chemical reactions can be described by writing down the atoms and molecules before and the atoms and molecules after. Since the atoms stay the same, the number

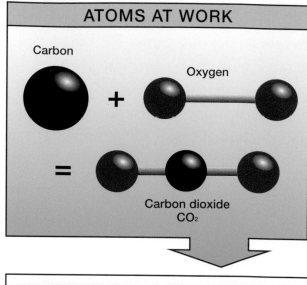

ATOMS AT WORK

Carbon

Oxygen

+

=

Carbon dioxide
CO_2

The chemical reaction that takes place when coal burns in air is written like this:

C + O$_2$ → CO$_2$

The number of carbon and oxygen atoms is the same on both sides of the equation.

of atoms before will be the same as the number of atoms after. Chemists write the reaction as an equation. This shows what happens in the chemcial reaction.

Making it balance

When the numbers of each atom on both sides of the equation are equal, the equation is balanced. If the numbers are not the same, something must be wrong. So the chemist looks at the equation again and adjusts the number of atoms involved until the equation balances.

When coal burns, a chemical reaction occurs between the carbon in the coal and oxygen in the air.

Glossary

acid rain: When certain gases rise into the atmosphere, they dissolve in rainwater, making the rain acidic.

allotropes: Different forms of the same element in which the atoms are arranged in a different pattern.

atom: The smallest part of an element that still has all the properties of that element.

atomic number: The number of protons in an atom.

bond: The attraction between two atoms that holds the atoms together.

carbon dating: A method of finding the age of old plant or animal material by measuring the amount of carbon-14 it contains.

cells: The building blocks from which plants and animals are made.

compound: A substance that is made of atoms of more than one element. The atoms in a molecule are held together by chemical bonds.

electron: A tiny particle with a negative charge. Electrons are found inside atoms, where they move around the nucleus in layers called electron shells.

fossil fuels: Fuels including coal, oil, and gas that formed from the bodily remains of prehistoric plants and animals.

greenhouse effect: Certain gases in Earth's atmosphere act like the glass in a greenhouse, trapping heat and stopping it escaping into space.

isotopes: Atoms of the same element that have the same number of protons and electrons but different numbers of neutrons.

metal: An element on the left of the periodic table. Metals are good conductors of heat and electricity.

molecule: A particle that contains atoms held together by chemical bonds.

monomer: A small unit or molecule. Monomers join up to form polymers.

neutron: A tiny particle with no electrical charge found in the nucleus of an atom.

nonmetal: An element at the right hand side of the periodic table. Nonmetals are liquids or gases at normal temperatures. They are poor at conducting heat and electricity.

nucleus: The center of an atom. It contains protons and neutrons.

periodic table: A chart of all the chemical elements laid out in order of their atomic number.

polymer: A long-chain molecule made up of hundreds or thousands of smaller units.

products: The substances formed in a chemical reaction.

proton: A tiny particle with a positive charge. Protons are found inside the nucleus of an atom.

reactants: The substances that react together in a chemical reaction.

Index